# The Last Map

# The Last Map

by

Art Zilleruelo

Published by Unsolicited Press
Portland, Oregon
www.unsolicitedpress.com

Editor: S.R. Stewart
Cover Art: Nathan Miller

For information, contact the publisher at
info@unsolicitedpress.com

Unsolicited Press Books are distributed to the trade by
Ingram.
Printed in the United States of America.
ISBN: 978-1-947021-03-7

# Contents

# I. Other Tongues

# Queen's English

This was not a cabin
to be sheltered in for one night
before simply returning to our old life.
We knew that,
somehow, going in.

We couldn't go back
to the Queen's English:
when, after a time, we found ourselves
back in town, we saw
the new words, and the new ways
of speaking the old ones,
reflected in friends' faces,
as they came to understand
that they were talking to the cabin.

What matters is the truth
we can speak to one other:
the truth of other crowns and other tongues,
of what poured in late that morning
through the cabin's windows,
when the blueberries burst in the oatmeal pot,
and put forth their color.

# Thread and Pixel

Light through a screen
door is frayed thread,
is thread legible to thread.

False texture of canvas:
a field made planar to the eye,
long liquid fibers

made landscape to the hand.
Light is livable fiction,
is map of mistakes,

and here in the edge-fray,
ragged thread and pixel-grain,
I float behind the teeth of things.

# Winter

Sing to us again of the winter
your grandmother crowned herself Empress
of Spain and Austria reunited in her person.

How she dragged her brocade train through snow,
wore the piss of wolves and cats
to inflame the passions of her cabinet.

How you entered the hall to flugel fanfare,
presented to the assembly as her dear Irish bog rat:
I recall you oily-haired in firelight,

playing quaint rustic fiddle
to the dinner guests.
Sing to us again.

# Diamond

Light woven into light
is wedding night rhetoric,
is cultivated diamond.

Braids tied to branch:
a knot between knuckles,
a noose to catch the moon.

I knew the moon once
in terms made obsolete
by their utterance.

The cut in the clouds a cut in the idiom,
a tongue split lengthwise
into light's divorced oracle.

# Lamb's Bones

Where do you need to believe yourself situated
in order for this exchange to unfold comfortably?

Let us embed you
in your richest memory:
summer, the Greek isles.

You told yourself and others
you were there on business,
and we'll grant that's not entirely untrue.

But let us insist upon
a little more transparency.

We've gathered that after an *agonia*
of deliberation, you resolved to accept
an invitation you thought of as "fraught."

But when you stumbled off the ferry
onto the starlit paths of Lemnos
to discover the *tavernes* closed
and the paved streets empty, you were half-
relieved to find the appointed place abandoned
and the invitation passively rejected,
as you knew it would be, if you waited.

And when the animal in you was activated
by the wandering scent of the roast,

when it lured you to the cove,
to the modest pit fire
where the lamb's bones cracked and smoked,
and the locals tolerated the intrusion
with mingled caution and hospitality,
you thought the only thoughts
that someone like you could think,
seated cross-legged on the sand
with smoke-stung eyes, tongue
aglow with ouzo and lamb.

But this is not then.
This is this. And here,
in what we hope will be
as gentle a revision as possible,
the ouzo has run out,
your hosts are absent,
and the only animation
on the beach's pale expanse is the fire,
where the lamb's bones cackled and spoke.

Your alarm at this stage is not unexpected;
neither are your inquiries.
But it must be said: we're asking the questions here,
and, in truth, supplying the answers.
Your role is to let the data
leak from you like liquid.

So, this is what happens next:
you'll hear a voice recite our translation
of what the lamb's bones said

14

as they burned, as they spoke to you in words,
and we'll study your face

as you listen, looking for something
we might know, if we see it.

# Kindling

What we wanted was light enough to lead us
in through the verge to the deeper copses
where the good kindling hid.

What we got were tone clusters
rising in weird vocation from the moss,
litterfall aglow with noise, or was it signal?

The crowns and limbs
were cold and high,
inert in weak winds.

I looked to you for confirmation or instruction,
but you had already taken your first steps in
without explanation or apology.

# Debriefing

Do you expect me to believe
that you emerged unchanged
from your time among the pines?

Had you walked out from under the canopy
bearing ancient beige headphones,
and crowned me with them,
and recited your account into the jack plug,
then, perhaps, I could have brought you home.

Or had I received an anonymous envelope
stuffed with cassette tapes, and unspooled
their ribbons to discover your argument,
such as it is, recorded in correction fluid
or white nail polish, I might have bitten at that lure.

But with nothing beyond your tongue's naked claims,
what choice do I have
but to plant you here, the moonlight spilling
truth into your hair, until you come clean,
or you change me to whatever you've become,
or we succumb to thirst together
and give the gift of our bones to this clearing?

# Vines

In a dream of driving,
you were beside me wondering aloud,
was I the man whose map could get you home?

That's when the veins swelled
in floods of ink beneath my map of skin
and bloomed through.

They were vines then,
black thorns and tendrils round the wheel,
writing us onto roads that no map knew.

You turned as I braked.
You'll want to get out of the car, I said,
till I get this thing figured out.

# The Worm

You cracked the moon when you beheld it,
and again when you named it.
The toothed worm resides inside the shell,

and is loosed to chew the tongue in two,
to flood new roads into the map,
to flatten history and cityscape.

But listen:
as I carved wards into mud with a birch twig,
as I warned you with desperate gesture
to stopper your word,

my tongue spilt its secret thirst,
and song-starved I opened my mouth
to the falling yolk of your errata.

# Birch Bark

A man could be forgiven
for thinking his days decreed
by secret itinerary scripted in birch bark,

and forgiven again
for carving cosmology
out of myths and folk physics,

but who among us could forgive himself
for finding down a dry well
in the corner of a coalyard

a rusty cutter, sharp enough to strip
each secret from the birch,
and casting it into the brown Susquehanna?

# Other Fires

Sure, there are other fires visible through the fog,
and paths that seem to lead in their direction.
But you walk past these things.

You read the bones of trout
suspended from the withies
on lengths of dental floss.

You keep the river far away,
so nothing but its own mouth
might swallow its petitions.

You plug your ears with mud
to learn the slow poems of elsewhere
from the ghosts the trees drank.

# Span

There is a hook that lives
in me, and any hand may tie
its line to the eye,
to reel me where it will,
to cast me out
in counterfeits of flight,
to tease a world of mouths
with intimations of a meal.

And I have learned through long repeat
the grammar of gravity,
the whiplash and the crash.

But in that span,
in the arc between the wrist's snap
and the impact,

I am sovereign in a blue country
and am food for nothing.

# Orchard

Do not ask
by what strange cost I came to learn this,
and do not ask who paid.

Deep in the earth's hot heart
resides a stag of animate granite,
who bears upon his molten rack
impaled remains:
ghosts like rags in wind,
flags in the blast of his breath.

His crown stabs paths through the globe,
boiling tongues etching poems in the dark,
until they publish through crust
and freeze in the light's climate.

These artifacts punctuate the grass
and are often mistaken for trees,
and my field for an orchard.

One day, on the cusp of a squall,
I found the neighbor girl
trespassing upon these grounds
with flagrant hair, and naked feet,
and appled breath, as with rude implements
she carved an epitaph.

Do not ask by what strange cost
I came to learn this,
and do not ask
who paid.

# Ashes

What was in the water
you woke the yeast with,
and what ashes in the hearth?

When and by what means
may I expect the return of my billfold,
cut and cured for me by a forgotten friend?

Crackling in the air above you:
somehow both a half moon
and a crescent.

What was in the cup
you soaked the stale bread in,
and why the lock without key or combination?

# The Alder

Red strobe of police presence
far over the hill's horizon,
where the sky drew confession from chimneys:

this is what woke me
with clay beneath my nails
and a pebble in my mouth.

I learned the dawn slowly
in the ways between town and wood
and braved a few paces into the treeline.

When I found your dress folded under the alder,
I followed my footprints out again
and took the sideroads home without you.

# Cartography

Light acquires wounds
on its way through a window,
emerges self-divorced from trials of geometry.

Bootprints trail off the map:
faded ink and rotten canvas,
history lost to the worm's thirst.

Dead center of all cartography,
the tongue acquires light,
swollen hell of swallowed maps,

fallen to luminous jewel,
spiral storm of stars,
temporary and terrible.

# II. Apocrypha Beatified

# Flowers of Bone

There is snow in the desert
that no doubt can melt.

A mouse moves
through it, unimpressed.

I am permitted within nine strides
before she turns to magic
brown stone, wrapped around a frantic heart.

I pause and my limbs are pale wood,
my hands are flowers of bone.

The blood comes quietly now,
and the breath.

For what threat could tree pose
to rock, or rock to tree?

A low voice insists:
wasn't there a well,
and wasn't she walking to it,
and didn't I follow?

But let it lie, for a tree
draws water from below,
and a stone needs none.

# The Pipe-Tree

I.
The story is:
late one sepia August,
having buried three stillbirths in as many summers,
my grandfather embarked for northern France,
landed at the Port of Gravelines,
procured axe and shovel of unique design,
and arranged carriage to a red x on a canvas map
he'd acquired through means we don't discuss.
There he drew a knot of roots
out of earth it shouldn't have been able to grow in,
and returned with it across an Atlantic torn by storms
in the last winter between the wars.

II.
When, precisely, he dragged this cargo
through his acreage to the three small plots,
and exhumed what slept there,
and laid it all down together
in the new bed he'd opened in the field,
no one can tell. Nor is it clear
how much of this procedure was known to his wife:
sometimes I picture her in sleep's black alibi;
others, I see her holding vigil in the kitchen,
tending the fire, and waiting with bucket and cloth
to wash him of the deed, and herself
of the urge to raise questions
neither could bear to hear answered.

III.
And what of that other vision, that lurid noir:
man and wife marching together in grim procession
to the site, their skin a pale scandal
in the mated light of the moon and the lantern,
their work in the dirt a prelude to some other rite?

IV.
And what of it? By spring there was a seedling
puncturing from below the late snow
that should have smothered it;
by summer, a sapling
whose clustered flowers wore
the color of honey, and the scent:
*Erica arborea*, our pipe-tree,
from which my grandfather harvested briar root
in only its fifth year, which he boiled in wine,
and dried on a bed of its own flowers,
before carving from it a thick-stemmed bowl
for smoking tobacco laced with honey and brandy
every night before retiring.
The next year, my father
came into the world, and stayed there.

V.
He and my mother were young when they met,
and still young when they married,
at my grandfather's insistence, under the shadow
of the pipe-tree, now tall, and black of trunk,
and laden with clutches of flowers
like pale yellow bells.

But I was the son of nobody's youth:
they'd wanted to conceive without assistance,
to refute what had blossomed
into the family's pet legend,
but my father begat nothing,
until he accepted the tutelage
willed to him and preserved in a yellowing envelope,
until he dug, and carved, and packed,
and took the heady blend
into his lungs and held it, and fell,
dizzy with it all, into my mother's embrace.

VI.
When the late spring storms
come in from the coast,
I can taste the smoke
in the wood and the walls,
and I feel this house's age
like stains in my joints.
I have now an Erica of my own;
she took my name
in some other field far north of here,
where the cold suffers no trees to grow.
We have come to see this place
through its long, last crumble, to walk our own path
to the graves lined up behind the tree,
close enough for the roots to reach,
and we'll carry no implements, we'll take nothing
from the earth, so as to owe nothing to it.

VII.

Families and their stories.
It falls to me to end this one.
My tongue is too familiar
with the past's gravity. I carry
what we all do. But I won't
breathe what burns, or plant in my wife's belly
the body that would grow
to shoulder my inheritance. I'll spare the tree,
but the envelope, the map, the pipes
of my fathers, I'll submit to the firepit's alchemy,
and watch from across the field
with wet scarves over my nose and mouth
as the ghosts rise, disguised as fire, as smoke,
as ash that can scatter in the weather
that comes across the ocean, calling its own name.

# Exploitation Cinema, Reel 1

In padlocked Vatican archives,
grainy handheld footage:
the Lady of Fatima

birthing a three-mouthed godthing
on a bed of dead militiamen,
entire navies of angels hovering in attendance.

Leaves fall flaming,
mothers kneel on debris
fingering rosaries and wailing for their sons,

forbidden gospel in pictures,
apocrypha beatified,
divinity housed in decayed frames.

# Lifted

Deer coupling on moonlit airstrips,
taxis abandoned at crossroads,
fuzzy dice dangling like glands from the rearviews.

Switchboards blinking pink protest and martyrdom,
halfhearted mobilizations of the somewhat prepared.
I watch an anchorman resign on-air,

watch myself dismantle phone jacks,
feel myself lifted to a disc of assembled starlight,
to passage through familiar underholes:

I'm a yawning wallet
pouring out penalties of birth debt
to a surgery I never elected.

# Strange Hours

Industry's dead in this town,
except when I'm trying to sleep.

But a man who keeps strange hours
and works soft jobs
can expect little sympathy here,
where one's time is so rarely one's own,
where words turn so often
to the colors of collars.

So I'm up now and moving
through fogs inside and out,
and I am needed nowhere
for some time, so I go
across the tracks to see
what peace might be made
with the rhythms of the forge,
with the accidental chords
of the trainyard's arrangement.

I have had days
in which the music of men's contraptions
moved me almost to outward display;
I have turned in silence
from a foreman who came to the fence
to inquire: what business
did I have here, and why would a man
be trembling in so warm an autumn,

and was there someone he could call
to come and drive me home?

But today's music eludes me.
The air offends: the incense of industry
like coins warmed in a wet palm.

So I cross back over the tracks
where morning meets the steam
of hot money, where the noise recedes,
if not into music, into atmosphere,
where I am a contrivance
of cold bones and jangling change
mere minutes from a cup of something warm,
where I am needed nowhere for some time.

# Sad Songs for Friends who Followed their Wallets out of Town

My friend,
I watched you sail on a bottlecap
out into forgetful countries.
Once a year I rent a scuba tank
and brush the ghost crabs from your hair.

My friend,
you left your spirit hanging
like an army of wet jackets
on the cactuses of Arizona.

My friend, fly home:
I'll fry you steak and eggs,
I'll chew for you
and spoon the pulp down on your tongue.

Every time the kettle sounds
you shut the door again, my friend.

My friend,
the heart beats false like a broken metronome,
the tooth falls soft and black,
awash in the crush of its pleasure dreams,
where are you?

My friend,
the sickles of your spat fingernails

wound my heels with remembrance.

My friend,
the flowers close themselves
against a world without you.

Don't worry, my friend:
I've been tending your garden,
canning the peppers,
and freezing the mint leaves.

My friend,
I've tracked your footsteps through the mountains,
but I can't follow into the pines.

My friend,
I keep my eyes low in summer,
and look to find you by your shadow.

My friend there is no one now
to iodine my minor wounds.

My friend,
if you're not back by January
I'm drinking your half of the scrumpy.

My friend,
I donated your clothes to the shelter,
then bought them all back the next day.

My friend,
the crickets scrape a song
of homecoming for you nightly.
I go to them at dawn
to keep the fishermen away.

Yes, my friend,
the ocean can swallow whole islands,
but I deny that it could ever swallow you.

My friend you have a way
of pushing a man to his limits.

My friend,
your alarm clock's off by an hour.
I confess to changing
the battery every spring.

My friend,
I see in the treetops at dusk
the silhouette of your ridiculous overbite.

I know your ways.
This joke is getting old, my friend.

My friend,
I find I can suffer the new weathers,
but only if I wear your overcoat.

# Forms

We'll call it *fall.*
We'll defer to old,
familiar forms of address,
but we'll feel the shock of the new
in this turning of these leaves,
in this cluster of dusks that darken
faster, purpler than their forebears.

And doesn't the sun find itself strained
more thinly through this year's clouds,
doesn't it look tired on the roof tiles,
its gold cut with enough air and time
to bleach it the yellow of runt corn?

We'll pronounce the miser syllable,
feeling its failure on lip, tooth, and tongue,
a hint of gag in the hollow vowel.

But we'll know it as we say it:
this cold and color shall suffer
no naming, we'll catch ourselves
conspiring like gossips against a guest
whose absence lends immunity to offense.

Until, caught in the long
shadows of the sugar maples, we beg
pardon: *so sorry, we didn't know
you were here.*

# Hallways

Raw data tore me out of bed
and gave me to the stars,
where I watched the city process life

in storms of algorithm,
while owls drank themselves woozy
on the humid drama of human souls.

Up there, the sickle of moon threatened surgery,
and what I prayed was lightning
or a ball of cryptic weather

wrote trademarks on the sky,
branded my sight with indecipherables,
and locked me in the hallways of its engines.

# Calculus

I no longer feel
as if each limb has been affixed
with cords of braided steel to a millstone.

Instead, I feel
as if every cell has had a molecule
in the shape of a millstone
suspended from it by a braid of atoms,
the total weight of which
burdens every limb with gravity
equal to that of the initial arrangement.

I'll answer before you ask:
this is change appreciable
to its system, a fresh affliction
with novel personality.

The forces at work here
dwell beyond the categories
of sums and parts.

For this domain is governed
by some other calculus.

Look: I lift a hand
to insult theory with anomaly:
the weight yielding for a moment
to a will inclining upwards,

here inside a physics
where things do not add up.

# Domain

Like all monuments, this one
undoes itself: here,
it would claim, is a logic
cast in rock, an argument
of rising momentum, totemic
epistle and savage rhetoric of state;
here, it would maintain, flies
a flag immune to the clouds' caprice,
history distilled and rendered steadfast
by strange arts, calcified slab of action
embalmed in the frozen humors of the earth.

But commemoration consigns its oratory
to memory's regime, delivers epiphany
into the domain of the epitaph,
archives occurrence
so we might meet it
and call it ours.

It would be possible, say the sages of the subatomic,
for me to press my palm to the fashioned surface,
for the emptiness in me and the emptiness in it
to align, for my blood and bone to enter into history,
to grasp the moment in the monument—
possible, but of probability so remote
that before my touch found its object,
the history it reached for would expire.

# We Know the Atom Consists Primarily of Empty Space

But when the knife enters the trout,
there is not enough nothing in the blade
to spare the gills, not enough nothing
in the bright blood to keep the bucket water clear.

# Mad Atoms

Yesterday I dared the city:
pity drove me to touch its wound,
to turn my fingerprints to evidence.

I know the real color of my alibi,
as does the moon,
drunk as she is on heart's data,

locked as she is with mad atoms.
I offered the driver of a taxicab
all the contents of my wallet

to drop me at a hospital;
he cursed me with the false violence of the surveilled
and left me crying under a lamppost.

# Provinces

Kitchen and bedroom become unknown
provinces, simple utensils are bent
to vague artifacts, the body itself

tailored into bespoke garments
for a client whose wealth is exceeded
only by his impatience,

when starlight finds you out
beneath the fever sheet,
below the blurred disc

of a ceiling fan,
above the quiet catastrophe
of bloodspots on the pillowcase.

# Exploitation Cinema, Reel 2

At a five-dollars-a-head basement talk,
three crackpot professors of forensics
fed the headshot into homebrewed software,

rendering black all but the cranial matter:
pixelated flesh aglow,
flowers of red radius and circumference,

a popped singularity of blood and bone
reconstituting as the footage rewound:
egg reshelled,

apple unbitten,
cosmos lifted to infancy
in the pictures of gravity's dream.

# Flowers

Monsignor smelled flowers
as he woke in strange radiance,
flowers in smoke

rising black from the hillside,
flowers on the hot wind
falling into fog,

flowers as he showed the tabloid correspondent
where angels descended on discs of cloud and flame
to lift a bleeding body,

where the dark ribbons rivered from the wounds,
raining redemption
down to ruined ground.

# Angel's Work

To the crow, it is all the same:
here, the wet remains
of a drive-thru bag;
there, the burst thing
that dragged itself curbside
in the moment before it stopped being life
and started being meat.

There's a touch of the chemist's logic
to this omnivore who knows
no dilemma: carbon is carbon,
origins mere trivia, and all things
are fuel for its engines,
all edible subjects fit study
for whatever black science
resides behind its eyes.

And is there not a holy note
to the rite over which the wings preside,
as the beak does articulate violence
to the feast that doubles as altar?

Is this not a species
of transubstantiation,
this conversion of garbage
to the fire that burns unseen
and propels the body skyward
into hunger's assumption?

Not chemistry, then,
but alchemy. Science
as it used to look:
like magic. For what else
but magic could account
for this agent of encyclopedic appetite
who scours the earth for all of the fallen,
and takes them into his secret ovens
where corruption is dissolved,
then mates them to the shape
that darkens the sky with angel's work?

# Exploitation Cinema, Reel 3

Every six months,
the widow of Signpost Road,
retired gentlewoman farmer,

receives a substantial sum
from an unknown party
for storing beneath the dirt

floor of her barn
a pair of lead-lined caskets,
a bucket of burned leaves,

and a stack of blue film canisters
corroded with red rust
and white mold.

# Zoological Gardens

Winter, and it is clear
to these caged awarenesses
that their keepers are not coming back.

Ground level,
the snow wears bruises:
the discharge of what's alive enough
to spray territories nothing
will ever threaten again.

The moon follows its orders
through snowstorms of stars,
while the wolves bend
to wolf-bones, and the elephants
exhume their dead
and tusk at them clumsily.

Flesh declines while snow flowers,
writing black space white
with reports of last diminishment,
erecting monuments to itself
with dead matter at the foundations,
marrying itself to the plexiglass
borders of the seal tank,
to the contours of the red plastic slide
someone once bought for the otters.

Hard to say if the snow knows
the world it has won.
Hard to say how long until
speaking of this world and the snow
as if they aren't the same thing
becomes an exercise in nostalgia:
arrayed beneath the heaps,
minor nodes of blue light
broadcast as the generators fail,
each pulse fainter than the last.

And then, the last.
As arbitrary, as inevitable
as any end.

Soon, everything that can eat
will have eaten everything,
and snow will fall unknown
to all but itself. Words will serve
the terms of their perjury
beneath the glass of dead wristwatches,
and I shall hush my spent tongue
less than halfway to the lake
I know I won't reach.

But for now, the snow
still owns me, and there is dying to do
and witness to bear.

I go under, to sing the wasted ribs
of the jaguar, the broken

beaks of the swan and the penguin,
as they meet their final fact
in silence, fixing themselves to stillness
to catch the song echoing down to them
through the frequencies of a dream,
through the emptiness that hides
like a promise
between the folds of fallen snow.

# Remember the Summer

The heart in this state resists
description, but here goes:

remember the summer we lost
an entire fridgeful to a blackout,

and while conducting the grim business
of rooting out the rot

we discovered in a corner
a forgotten bowl of oats,

gone green beneath plastic wrap
and knuckled with black globes,

the fruit of our neglect,
ripe and dark as a dead fist?

We bagged it and binned it with the rest,
but it had entered through my nose

and settled in a hollow
where its color has grown audible:

apply your cheek to my chest and hear it
there, and there, and again there,

the ghost of a punch haunting its halls,
sounding out the only word it knows.

# Anniversary Card

I would watch every constellation fall derelict,
and every galaxy dissolve in the stomach of another,
and all of space shudder and freeze and crack at the
        seams,
and still I wouldn't leave the shadow of this tree without
        you.

# Atlas

I awoke to discover the horizon
had acquired a spine.

Next, as if weary of the wounds
done to its reputation
by generations of cartographers,
the world folded in upon itself
along that terrible hinge,
collapsing into its own atlas.

I should have ended
as rude ink shared between pages,
but there was space enough,
and grace, in that topography
to offer me asylum.

I wander now through a wordless volume,
taking nourishment from its leaves and living dyes,
reading its body with my hands, lungs, and tongue,
and teaching things the secrets
of their own rearrangement:


from my seat atop a peak,
I touch a sky made of a lake's skin,
and close a circuit, and my bones become
the channel through which these pages read

their opposites, through which this water talks
for the first time to this rock,
in the slow tones of the last map.

# Brylcreem Harmonies

My worst fears come true:
I am right about everything,
and the night breaks

under lunar and stellar mandate,
oceans pour in through the fissures,
jellyfish wither the clouds with their glow.

On the beach, fires to eat the floating dead.
From the radio on the sand altar,
the Brylcreem harmonies of the last surviving hymns,

and the waves of static cresting out and out
into the breakers, into a blonde body
chasing the future as it dies.

# New Greens

Wind has always been
a stone to me,
a monolith of clear weight
I negotiate with patience.

Until today,
when the stone melted,
chewed somehow into my boot,
cut a hole through which to worm,
set teeth to tissue,

and sent me running
to tell the world what it already knows
of wolves and flowers,

to stop in the pale oak's shadow,
to watch it steep the sun's gold
and the sky's blue
in the crucible of its heart's knot

and brew and bleed new greens into the grass.

# III. Fool's Fire

# Ghost Story

In a field near the lake
stands the ghost of a dead oak.
The ghost is black and very tall.
It never speaks or moves.
The sky wants to take it.
The earth wants to eat it.
But the ghost is strong, it does not want to move.
So it argues half its tongues into the dirt,
and grips hard against the sky's glutton lung.
It whispers the other half into air,
and weathers the white earth's thirst.
Like a frayed black suture
it binds earth and sky together.
In this way the ghost stills its universe:
the sky can never rise nor the earth fall
out of their coupling's grave jurisdiction.
The lake will breathe its atoms to the clouds.
The constellations will pageant
the lucky patterns of their composition
until they break and fade.
But the ghost will stand
contented with the silence.
With the snowfall.
With the stalemate of its own device.

# Sigil

I.
Either the friction of voice
or the scraping of wind on wood:

words were falling in leaf form—
whether into me or out
I can't say,

or won't—
and anyway, once the tongue's inside the ear
what's the difference?

This much is certain:
leaves were calling in flame form,
small life was rooting in snow,
steam rose in weird rain,
you were there.

II.
But not in any sense that mattered.
What sun there was hung grey with vague anger:
a milk sphere of cataract.
I learned to look unblinking,
and from the burn emerged a sigil to decipher.
In this way I welded you into my science
and followed you like fool's fire through the world.

III.
You resisted all search.
I learned to look again,
where the snow lay unbroken,
and the trees' frozen history
did not include your touch.
And in that pathless expanse,
I read your cruel riddle
and felt you somehow with me, I was lonely.

IV.
These proximities I feared and fled:
I needed to know myself far from you.
I wanted to feel the folklore.
But these were wanting days:
I stripped birch bark and chewed out the oils,
brewed evil teas with sick grass,
traded confessions with the air,
whistled dumb male arias of regret,
pissed history in the snow,
and consigned it by the fistful to the fire.

V.
In a wind that spanned oceans,
I clung to the bowing bones of the oak;
in spiral and turbulence,
new flesh from other waters
fell like the veins of a galaxy,
inclining to a central question,
like a voice upon my ears and mouth
as I pulled the shreds of leaf out.

VI.
This crush, this curtain,
vales appalling of female storm,
neither the fiction of choice
nor the scripture of signs in flood.

VII.
Scribbled character,
talisman illegible,

I ask for little,
and usually for nothing,
but if ever I drew you fleshways out of history,

listen:
just call me out of the poem.

# Summons

I.
I have made it my custom not to go
outdoors past nightfall anymore,

yet if you were to rise now
and answer the window's summons,

if you were to part your curtains and admit
the mingled spill of moon and star,

you would discover me down on the bricks,
taking a knee before a curious thing:

a triangle, equilateral, rendered in yellow chalk,
its vertices intersecting the perimeter
of a circle of lamplight, with a point

whose gravity makes a satellite of me:
a brass tack driven into the circumcenter,
burnished, flickering pupil of an implied eye.


II.
You would register the spine's inclination,
the quick shiver as the notion takes me,
as I let myself be drawn

closer, lower, to the lip of that event

horizon, as I watch my figure swell
and fill that mirror till it drinks me,

till I discern as through a fisheye lens
a bent countenance: author of the whole
contingent arrangement, who numbers

among the materials
that populate his open studio
the light, the air, and time,

and who, perhaps,
watches from some other window
as I seek him in the surface of a pin's head.


III.
Or would you watch me knock upon a devil's door,
hear me call a denizen of elsewhere
to come and pull me under,

and let her tongue drip its liquor
into my gasp, and plant its gift in me,
and dive with her hand round my wrist

through lightless waters,
through crust and mantle,
down to her bed of burning words?

IV.
If you were to rise now
and summon the window's answer,

if you were to discover me
surrendered to hollow talk,

uncertain of my part
in the trial of grave angles,

I would lift the yellow-petaled gifts
of the brick's periphery,

I would administer
through moon-stained lips

the spell of mangled stars
to the light, the air, and time,

and let myself be drawn aloft on questions:
*Is this what we are?  Are we flowers?*

# Arrangements

No family. Anything but that
distributed wave of same
blood, different bodies.

No friends. Let them find some other
pretext for hauling out the secret ledger,
for declaring one of their own
eliminated by the math.

Only our lawyer,
tramping through a field
with a napkin map,
a spade, and two parcels,

stopping in the shadow of an oak
to dig, to unfold and upend,
to pack the dirt down hard
over our last bed.

# The Leaves

Knowledge of the end
infects this house
like an atmosphere of incense,
and makes our tangled breath a dirge.

6:66 A.M. when the watch dies:
a minute that breathes
beyond the reach of hands,
a minute that can never come to pass,
and can therefore never end.

Have you ever felt
your heart match the second hand?
They breathe together a moment,
then divorce.

If my breath is the first to break,
I'll wait for you at the lake,
and meet you where the leaves put down their stain.

# Acknowledgments

Earlier versions of "Thread and Pixel," "Diamond," "The Worm," and "Cartography" first appeared in *New Fraktur Arts Journal*.

Earlier versions of "Lifted," "Exploitation Cinema, Reel 2," "Evil Maths," "Mad Atoms," and "Provinces" first appeared in *Petrichor Machine*.

"We Know the Atom Consists Primarily of Empty Space" and "Ghost Story" first appeared in *James Dickey Review*.

"Brylcreem Harmonies" first appeared in *Thumbnail*.

An earlier version of "Zoological Gardens" first appeared in *The Cincinnati Review*.

"Sigil" first appeared in *Vector*.

"Atlas" first appeared in *Phantom Drift*.

The following poems were collected and published as the chapbook *Weird Vocation*, from Kattywompus Press: "Thread and Pixel," "Diamond," "The Worm," "Cartography," "Sad Songs for Friends who Followed their Wallets out of Town," "Orchard," "We Know the Atom Consists Primarily of Empty Space," "Domain," "Zoological Gardens," "New Greens," "Anniversary Card," "Kindling," "Vines," "Birch Bark," "Other Fires," "Ashes," "Winter," "The Alder," "Ghost Story," "Sigil," and "Summons."

# About the Author

Art Zilleruelo received an MFA from Wichita State University and a PhD from Northeastern University. He is the author of *The Last Map* (Unsolicited Press, 2017) and *Weird Vocation* (Kattywompus Press, 2015).

# About the Press

Unsolicited Press was founded in 2012 and is based in Portland, Oregon. The team seeks to produce phenomenal poetry, fiction, and nonfiction. Learn more at www.unsolicitedpress.com.

www.ingramcontent.com/pod-product-compliance
Lightning Source LLC
Chambersburg PA
CBHW051433090426
42737CB00014B/2957